how to have a
grand
&
glorious
relationship

Brett Neil

Published by Motivation Champs

Special discounts may apply on bulk quantities.

Please contact Motivation Champs Publishing to order www.motivationchamps.com

ISBN Paperback 978-1-956353-62-4

ISBN Hardcopy: 978-1-956353-60-0

ISBN Ebook: 978-1-956353-61-7

Contents

Dedication 1

Introduction 3

Foreword 9

Chapter 1: Choose Wisely 13

Chapter 2: No Longer About Me 19

Chapter 3: Understand Each Other 23

Chapter 4: Encourage Each Other 27

Chapter 5: The 3 Relationship "F Words" Friendship,
Freedom and Forgiveness 35

Chapter 6: Learn to Say "No" 41

Chapter 7: Be Kind 45

Chapter 8: Be Generous 49

Chapter 9: Be Truthful 55

Chapter 10: Fight Fair 59

Chapter 11: Learn to Laugh 63

Chapter 12: Keep It Fresh 67

Chapter 13: Take care of yourself! 73

Conclusion 79

About the Author 83

Dedication

I hope we all have people in our lives who inspire us to be better and pursue our goals. One of the people who inspired me to write was my high school English teacher, Mrs. Ray.

For years, she wrote a weekly piece in the Adrian Journal, telling inspiring stories, and encouraging people to be kind and trust God. When the paper closed down, she began publishing her "Story of the Week" on Facebook. I look forward to them each Monday!

She taught for 30 years at Adrian High School. Each day of every month, she prays for one of her old classes, enabling her to cover them all every 30 days. There is no doubt she truly cares for all her kids.

In speech class, I would sometimes volunteer to give my speech first. Not because I was prepared but because that would give me an opportunity to write my speech after I gave it.

On my 60th birthday, my sister Deb gave me some papers from Mrs. Ray. Apparently, she was going through some old papers and found something I had written back in '75 or '76. It was truly Pulitzer material. I understand why she kept it for so many years! When she heard it was my birthday, she sent it with Deb to give me. What a wonderful gesture. It reminded me how much I enjoyed writing and how, as a kid, I dreamed of writing for the New Yorker.

Mrs. Ray, thank you for your encouragement to me and the countless others you have inspired over the years. May God bless and keep you healthy and strong for years to come.

I love you, Brett

Introduction

The idea for this book came about through a T-shirt I had made after I wrote my book *Have a Grand and Glorious Day*. It looks like this.

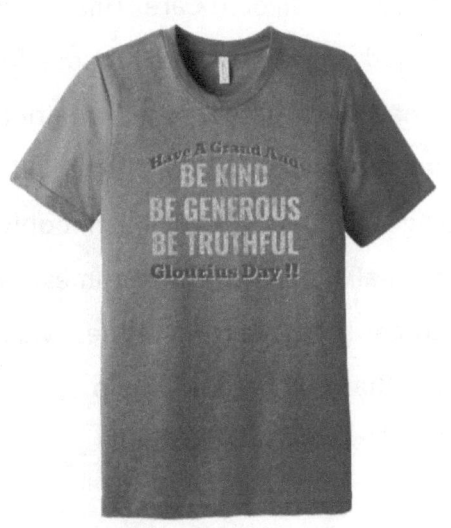

People often come up to me and tell me how much they like the shirt and its message. Being kind, being generous, and being truthful are things that, deep down, appeal to all of us regardless of race, religion, gender, or age. My "happy place" is helping people improve their lives. I love seeing people grow in their relationships, careers, and spiritual walks. I know that with just a few disciplines, these things are possible. My goal is to spend the rest of my days leading people to live free of fear and anxiety in all areas of their lives.

The content of this book is based on things I have learned over the years while helping couples prepare for marriage and leading Divorce Care. This summer, a friend asked me if I had an outline he could use for premarital counseling. I had been gathering information for several years, and I felt led to write a book that could be useful for people of all ages and all walks of life, not only in marriage but in all relational areas of life. Sometimes, we just need a little nudge to get going, and his request was the nudge I needed. I hope that this book will help you find and grow your Grand and Glorious Relationship!

Learning to live in harmony with those around us should be the focus of our lives. It is both rewarding and, I believe, our obligation to live at peace with each other. I don't care what your religious belief is or if you even have one; our instinct tells us that loving and respecting each other is the right thing to do. Hopefully, this book will help you learn ways to do so. No matter your position or vocation, treating others with kindness, generosity, and truthfulness will contribute greatly to your overall happiness. Each morning, as you get ready to take on the world, I hope you will focus on these traits and make them a habit over time. I believe there are tidbits of information that will help people of all ages with relational skills. I have learned that it is pretty easy to get along with most people, if we are willing to put just a little effort into it.

While this book's primary focus is directed at romantic relationships, I have found that most of the disciplines can also be applied to our personal and business relationships.

Each year, for the past 15 years, I have chosen a word representing an area of my life that I want to focus on and improve. My word for 2024 is the Koine Greek word poneros, which is translated as "evil" in Latin-based bibles, but literally means labors, annoyances, and hardships. Words matter. The correct interpretation makes all the difference in the world. This is a perfect example. In what we refer to as the Lord's prayer, our English translations read, "lead us not into temptation but deliver us from evil." The Koine Greek reads, "lead us not into temptation but deliver us from labors, annoyances and hardships." I'm convinced that most problems that weigh us down are self-inflicted. My prayer is that this book will point you in a direction that will help you avoid labors, annoyances, and hardships as much as possible. Life is short. The more we can avoid self-inflicted wounds, the happier we will be.

My wife and I will celebrate 45 years of marriage this year. It has been a great marriage. We are blessed. We have worked hard at it. Many of the principles I will share we stumbled upon accidentally, and some we learned from others successes or mistakes. I am confident that if these principles are practiced, the chance for a happy relationship is greatly increased. There are no shortcuts to lasting success in any area of life. This is especially true in relationships.

I am grateful that you are willing to take the time to read this book. I hope that when you are finished, you will let me know what you think!!! I look forward to hearing from you.

The following is a conversation between my 7-year-old grandson and I.

Jude: How old are you?

Me: 65

Jude: How old is Mimi?

Me: 63

Jude: So if everything goes right, you should die first?

Me: Yes that sounds fair. I think MiMi will live to be an old, old woman because I have taken such great care of her. What do you think?

Jude: I don't know. I'm not always around you, but when I am all I see you doing is hugging and kissing her!

Foreword

I want to make it clear that although I believe this book will be of great help to many couples of all ages who are entering into a long-term relationship, it can also help those of us who are already in one. Relationships that last and grow are hard work. There are many challenges that come along. The way we handle them can make our relationships fruitful or dry them up. Every relationship I have observed could be better with a little effort. My hope is that this book will challenge each of us to strive to be a better us for our partners.

As I mentioned, my wife, Linda, and I will celebrate our 45th anniversary this year. We have been blessed with two sons, four grandchildren, and a wonderful daughter-in-law, and we are looking forward to another daughter-in-law and more grandchildren. Looking back, I can honestly say I would do it all over again and wouldn't change a thing other than try to be a little kinder. I would not change anything major because I realize if I did, that would affect something else, which would mean I would not be where I am now. The place I would be might be better, or it might be worse. I'm content to be right here doing my best to enjoy the now. I have learned that while we are waiting for life to happen, we miss out on it.

My dad died when I was three. My mom remarried when I was six. My stepdad and I had a rocky relationship at times. Looking back, I realize it was probably mostly due to my insecurities. I was the youngest of seven. My siblings all had many memories of my Dad. I had three: one of him in the hospital, one of him on the couch in our home, and one of my Uncle Wylie holding me at the funeral home in front of the casket. I remember asking him why people were crying and why they weren't happy to see Daddy.

Although Bob was very good to my mom and me, I think I never really felt the freedom to let go of my dad and look at Bob as Dad. In fairness I don't think Bob felt that freedom either. I remember asking him once if I could call him Dad, and he told me no. My guess is that it wasn't because he didn't love me but because he was also insecure about how that would be perceived by the rest of the family. Either way, we had our ups and downs, but I am eternally grateful for the times we had and for the way he loved my Mom and our family. He taught me, by example, how to step up and help around the house.

It is my belief that most of us, deep down, want to be in a viable relationship. The problem is, for many, we don't know how and are intimidated by all of the failed relationships around us. We have seen our parents, our friends, our coworkers, people from all walks of life, religious people, and non-religious people—it doesn't seem to matter— struggle and fail at relationships, and we are beginning to wonder if it is possible to make a relationship last. I know it is possible, and the purpose of this book is to share a few proven actions that can make a great relationship a reality.

There will be some who read this book and think I am naïve and believe in fairytale endings and Fantasy-Land relationships; I assure you I do not. I have been blessed with a wonderful marriage. It has been a blast, and I would do it all over again, but this does not mean it has always been easy. We have had moments of stress, conflict, and disagreements, and we still do. We have endured and flourished because of many of the principles in this book, some of which we practiced by choice and others we stumbled upon by dumb luck.

It is very important that every person reading this book knows I judge no one. Jesus said He did not come to judge, and His Father did not, so I sure have no business judging anyone. The purpose of this book is to help each of us make our lives a little easier by making our relationships a little better. My hope is that people of all ages will find a few "nuggets" to help them be a little better partner.

Chapter 1

Choose Wisely

For over 40 years, I have been involved in marriage and crisis counseling strictly on a layman basis. I do not have any formal training in the area, but I have countless hours in the trenches with real people, helping them navigate through marriage, divorce, and breakups. I led Divorce Care for several years. During that time, I witnessed all kinds of heartbreak stories. The hurt and pain from broken relationships is excruciating. One constant in their stories was that deep down, they knew they had not chosen wisely in the beginning.

We will touch on choosing wisely several times throughout the book. Sometimes it seems as though people put more thought into choosing a dress or a set of golf clubs than choosing a partner. Taking time to evaluate and choose wisely is key to having a great relationship or for making any important decision. In this chapter, I want to look at a few ways to help you do that. I also want to point out that if you are already in a marriage in which you didn't choose wisely, it is still possible to have a thriving relationship, but it will mean you have to put some extra effort into building a healthy, lasting relationship.

Here are a few of my suggestions. First of all, I am a believer in love at first sight. I'm not saying it happens that way for everyone, but I know it is that way more often than not in long-lasting, fun, healthy relationships. I can still remember the first time I "saw" my wife 48 years ago in the hallway of Adrian High School! As I walked up the stairway to class, I was immediately smitten. Deep down, I don't think I ever doubted that she was the person I wanted to spend the rest of my life with. That sentiment has never changed. I can still sit across the room from her and just be amazed by her beauty.

I am convinced that healthy infatuation can overcome a lot of disagreements. I want to clarify what I mean when I refer to healthy infatuation. I am not talking about an infatuation that leads you to be a creepy stalker but rather an emotion that literally mesmerizes you when you are with that person. There is an old saying that beauty is in the eye of the beholder. When you look at the person you are in a relationship with, you should marvel at their beauty inside and out. If you don't, I would question the sustainability of your relationship.

Love or lust alone is not enough to make a personal relationship last and be fun. Love is a choice. Healthy infatuation is a feeling or desire. I can choose to love someone even if we don't have much in common. It is a deliberate decision to care for them even when, on occasion, I may not like them! Healthy infatuation is not something you decide to do; it's just there.

A relationship cannot last without love; it cannot thrive without infatuation! I know many people who have been in a relationship for years because of making that choice to love, sometimes out of obligation, however, it is obvious that there's not much physical attraction there. Infatuation is what keeps a marriage fun and exciting! Love without infatuation is enduring but without as much laughter and joy.

Again, I am talking about healthy infatuation, not obsession.

Secondly, you must ask questions while you are dating and before you get in too deep. This is not a suggestion; it is not optional but mandatory if you want to ensure your relationship has the best possible chance of succeeding. It is also important not to let your infatuation dominate your common sense. If it does, you are probably dealing with obsession or desperation instead of healthy infatuation.

It is imperative that you discover what is important to each other. Asking questions is one of the best ways to get to know someone. Another suggestion I have is to get pre-engagement counseling. Premarital counseling is usually too late. Here are a few questions you should ask each other before getting engaged.

- How do you view marriage?
- Is it something you want?
- What do you want your marriage to look like?
- What role do you see yourself and your spouse playing in the marriage?
- What do you see in the other person's work ethic?

- How do you relate with your immediate family? How do they relate to theirs?
- Do you want kids? If so, how many?
- Are you a spender or a saver?
- How do you view debt?
- How much debt do you have?
- Are you comfortable taking responsibility for the other person's debt?
- Do you have good credit?

Finances need to be discussed because they are one of the major causes of divorce, yet it is a subject that nearly every couple I have worked with over the years has either never discussed or just brushed over before getting deeply involved. Money practices tell a lot about a person's character. I understand we can all fall on occasional bad times. The thing to look for is repeat issues. Responsible finances are a lot like love. It is a choice of behavior.

Thirdly, you need to spend time together with each other's family and friends. Pay attention to the interaction. More than likely, the person you are dating will, at some point, treat you the way they treat their family. Listen to their conversations and watch their facial expressions. Ask your family and friends what they think. Encourage them to be honest with you. If you receive negative feedback, take note. If the majority of your family and friends are negative or non-committal about the relationship, you should take notice. Life is too short to get tied down in a relationship that is probably doomed from the beginning.

Lastly, observe the person's character. Do they tip well? Do they work hard? Are they polite to you and others? Do they jump in and help others or sit and watch? Do their friends trust them? Do you trust them? Are they generous, truthful, and kind? Are they dependable? Do they show up on time? Are they there when you need them?

What about you? You should ask these same questions of yourself. All fair questions apply to both parties. As you are seeking answers to these questions from others, examine yourself. Be honest in your self-evaluation. I understand that as we mature, we can improve in all of these areas; however, if a person is selfish, lazy, stingy, and rude now, they probably aren't going to change later.

Infatuation with the wrong person will fade. Love can often overcome many faults, but choosing wisely is the best way to ensure both lasting infatuation and love.

Chapter 2

No Longer About Me

If I am determined to build a lasting relationship, I must come to grips with the fact that from this day forward, it is no longer just about me; it is about us. To build a relationship with someone who will endure the tough times in life, the other person must trust that my decisions will have their best interest (as well as mine) in mind. No relationship can thrive if I am selfish and make decisions without considering the well-being of the other person.

This principle is true in dating, marriage, raising kids, friendships, and business. I, and no one else, can be secure in a relationship unless I know the other person has my back. If I live in fear or doubt that when I enter a relationship, the other person may choose to do what is best for them at my expense without considering the consequences for me, I will not be comfortable in the relationship.

In a dating relationship, it is important to make sure the other person knows what I am looking for in life and vice versa. Although our hobbies and interests might differ, our views of ethics, family structure, children, retirement, etc., need to be on a similar page. As you date, think about these things. Be open and honest. Ask questions. Learn about the other person's past and present, relationships, family, work history, friendships, and beliefs.

Knowing someone's "story" is very helpful in under-standing their present and, in many ways, their future. While our past does not have to determine our future, it does shape or influence how we look at life in general. For instance, if I had an abusive father, becoming a loving father myself would probably not come naturally to me. It doesn't mean I can't be one, but I will likely need help learning how to be one. Knowing my childhood experience could also help those around me understand why I think and see things the way I do. Thankfully, I had two older brothers, some wonderful neighbors, and a stepfather to give me direction. They loved me, and each one taught me different things about life. Still, I never knew the joy or security of being held in my father's arms. I can only imagine what it might have felt like; maybe it would have been totally different than my preconceived perception, but as a father, I was determined to make sure my kids and grandkids would never miss out on knowing what it was like to be held and told how much they were loved.

One of the best ways I have found to change how I think and act is with little reminders. For me, that means notes on my dash, my monitor, and anywhere I can see them to help me remember. I also like to memorize a sentence or two that I can repeat to myself each time I am reminded about the subject. I try to replace these notes often and relocate them to keep them fresh. If I don't, they become part of the landscape, and I ignore them. I try to keep the notes or thoughts short and to the point. For example, on the subject of thinking about others, I would say, "I always choose what's best for us, not just me." It has been proven many times that what we believe about ourselves will control how we act. It's imperative that I do everything within my power to build up my self-esteem and confidence. We only get one shot at this life. It's up to me to decide what my life will look like. No one can change me but me. I have to take responsibility for my actions and attitude. Once I do, I am able to live a life of joy and abundance when it comes to relationships.

Chapter 3

Understand Each Other

As you enter into a relationship, you must learn to understand the needs of the person you are with. Men and women are different. Our physical and emotional needs cause us to look at things differently, and we require different types of confirmations to fulfill them.

Taking time to find out what fulfills your partner's needs is time well spent. If I learn the things that help my partner feel comfortable and appreciated, it is highly likely they will do the same for me.

My wife loves flowers. She loves some more than others. Once, as a gift, I had flowers delivered to our home on the first Wednesday of each month for a year. While she appreciated them, I soon learned she would have been happier being surprised with two or three arrangements of her favorite flowers spontaneously delivered throughout the year rather than getting a dozen arrangements on a specified day of the month for a year. Honestly, as I look back on it, the flowers were not nearly as important as the act of showing her from time to time how much I love her and appreciate what she means to me.

Men, on the other hand, need verbal confirmation. A verbal acknowledgment or praise gives a man a desire to do more. Constantly bringing up past mistakes will typically create bad results rather than good ones. Men have an innate ability to block out perceived nagging and an even greater ability to live up to your opinion of them. If you build them up, they will tend to do better, but if you tear them down and remind them how rotten they have been in the past, they won't disappoint.

Learning to take time to see a situation from the other person's point of view takes discipline. I'm not saying I change my mind every time I listen to someone else's point of view. I do, however, at least understand where they are coming from and can try to see things from their point of view. Whether we can agree on a solution is yet to be seen, but at least we both know we are listening. There is nothing wrong with agreeing to disagree. There doesn't always have to be a winner or a loser. A relationship is not a sporting event; it is a partnership, and in a partnership, there has to be room for disagreement.

Comedian Yakov Smirnoff has put together what might be the most impressive piece of work on relationships I have ever seen. I highly recommend researching it for anyone in a relationship or wants to be in one. One of the things he points out is that laughter is one of the key elements to a lasting healthy relationship. Understanding each other helps us be able to laugh. We will be too serious if we don't know where each other is coming from. Laughing together releases tension, which in turn brings down barriers. Most of what we fight about is caused by misunderstandings; therefore, we end up not meeting each other's needs.

Chapter 4

Encourage
Each Other

Adults and children alike need to be encouraged. We all need to know we have purpose and value. For years, I wondered what my purpose was. I kept waiting for some big sign or revelation about what I was here for. Eventually, I realized that all of us have the same purpose: to love God and our neighbor as ourselves. It doesn't really matter what my vocation is; the only thing that will last and make this life Grand and Glorious is how I handle my relationships.

One of my daily encouragements to myself is the following: "God created me in His image to reflect His life, light, and love. I have purpose and value, or I would not be here. Nothing can stop me from fulfilling my purpose but me, and I am not going to let that happen!" This is also something I use to encourage others. We are all valuable and have purpose. Most people are unhappy because they don't believe they have value and purpose, many because they have never been told, and others because they have always been told just the opposite.

We all like to be encouraged, but most of us seem to have a hard time being the encourager. You will find people who encourage each other's dreams in a good relationship. We all have dreams and things we would like to do. We strengthen our bond by encouraging our partner and showing interest in their dreams.

We need to spend our lives trying to be a better "me." Too many people are trying to become someone else. You are who you are for a reason. Focus on becoming the best you can be. To get better, we need encouragement. Few people grow from constant negative input.

In a relationship, you need to be the one constant encouragement your partner can count on and vice versa. We can't become what we need to be if you don't become what you need to be. Two people can't be happy together if they are not happy individually. You should be your partner's encourager for self-preservation if for no other reason! When your partner in life is happy and fulfilled, there is an excellent chance you will be, too!

Never criticize your partner in front of others. Always stand up for them and speak kindly of them. Nothing cuts deeper than hearing your partner put you down in front of your peers. Wounded spirits are hard to heal. Be careful of how you speak. We need to joke and laugh at ourselves, but we should be careful not to go too far and ridicule or embarrass each other in public.

When you and your partner are alone is the time to challenge each other: Challenge, not attack. There are times we need to know, in kindness and truth, that we were a jerk or out of line. We all need to know when something we said or did was rude or hurtful. As humans, there are times when we say or do things, and we don't realize the hurt we caused or the boundaries we crossed. Many a time over the years, my wife has needed to call me out about something I've said or done because I was oblivious to it. I am totally fine with this, even though I don't always like to hear it.

Constructive criticism is great as long as it really is constructive. However, many of my experiences with what was presented as constructive criticism by others have turned out to be negative because, in reality, it was just criticism with no purpose other than the person presenting it resented that I dared disagree with them.

For many, constructive criticism means, "Let me air my grievances and rip you a new one!" This is not constructive. I've found it's best to leave the words "constructive criticism" out of a conversation. Some words are "trigger" words. These two definitely fit that description.

It's better to say, "You know you were wrong tonight," or "You need to think about your response to your mom." A kind, truthful statement is better than a two-hundred-word lecture on the situation! Every person needs to be encouraged. Each of us has good days and bad. We all need someone to lift us up and help us believe we can accomplish our dreams, overcome obstacles, or sometimes just survive the day.

I love people with positive attitudes. I love being that person. I wish I could say I was always positive, but I have to admit, some days I am not! Those are the days I need an encourager, someone who will gently remind me that 1. Things probably aren't as bad as they look and 2. Tomorrow is a new day.

Encouragement is vital in a relationship. Couples or partners who encourage each other seem to thrive. Lack of encouragement or the presence of discouragement will cause a wounded spirit. As Solomon said, "A man can endure sickness, but who can endure a wounded spirit?"

I want you to understand that this book is about intimate relationships. When I speak of a wounded spirit, I refer to how a person feels when someone they trust betrays them. I am not talking about the current trend of "you can't do that because I'm offended." I'm afraid we are allowing a generation of people, young and old, to be free of a difference of opinion because it hurts their feelings. Differences of opinion are what make us strong.

The idea of "iron sharpens iron" is that two differing opinions make us stronger when we openly and honestly converse. Demanding that everyone agree with me is ridiculous. I see it happening in our government, schools, and churches. I truly believe it is the greatest threat our nation faces today. You cannot have unity if you do not allow differing opinions. I am going to say that again. You cannot have unity if you do not allow differing opinions. I know that sounds strange, but think of it this way: there are no two people who believe exactly the same way; we are all different; we may agree on 90% of the same things, but we will differ on some.

Unity is caused by differing opinions, compromising, and finding common ground we can agree upon. If I know my opinion or concern does not matter to someone, we are no longer united but at odds with each other. In social settings, we can literally become enemies instead of just two people who don't see eye to eye on everything. Over the past few years, our politicians and the "elite," with the help of the media, seem to have been able to convince us that we have to hate everyone different than us. We don't notice how they are taking advantage of their power as long as they can keep us fighting against each other.

The point is that we will never be 100% on the same page, so get over it, talk it through, and don't run home to mommy every time someone tells you no or that you are wrong. Instead, stop and reflect on what they said. You might find you were wrong, and you need to make a change.

Thanks for allowing me to chase that rabbit! Now, back to encouragement. Taking time to let our partner know that we noticed something they did for us or are aware of their unique talents is encouragement. Reminding them of their gifts and positive traits can be huge when they are discouraged. I don't care how positive we are; sometimes we consider giving up. Those are the times, more than ever, in which we need to step in and build up. I need to be my partner's biggest fan. The benefits are amazing!

Chapter 5

The 3 Relationship "F Words"

Friendship, Freedom and Forgiveness

I n addition to love and infatuation, three other areas are vital to a healthy relationship.

The first of these would be friendship. In the American Heritage Dictionary, friendship is defined as a "person whom one knows, likes, and trusts." If you don't genuinely like the person you are in a relationship with, you are going to have some tough times.

I can honestly say Linda is my best friend. We love to spend time together. We enjoy traveling, going to movies, hanging out in the pool, and spending time with our family. We are content being with each other; in fact, we look forward to it. She is definitely someone I know, like, and trust. I can't imagine life without her.

Even though we are best friends, we have hobbies, interests, and friends we enjoy separately. Linda loves to decorate and work in the yard with her flowers. She likes to shop, go to lunch with friends, take trips with her mom and others to Branson, Canton, and anywhere else they sell things!

I like to golf. I look forward to getting out with my friends, my sons, my grandson, and once in a while, by myself. Golfing, for me, is a great tension reliever. A little music on the speaker, and I could play for hours.

I enjoy getting away for a few days occasionally and spending some time off the grid. I like to hunt, fish, and camp. Being out in nature on the boat, in the tent, or in the woods with no phone recharges my battery.

Thankfully, I'm not much on decorating and shopping, and Linda's not much on golfing and camping. This brings us to the second "F word": Freedom.

To keep a relationship fresh and exciting, we all need some time to do the things we enjoy without feeling guilty about it. Over the years, I have seen a lot of couples struggle in this area, usually because it's a one-way street.

Sorry guys, but typically, I see men use the stress of their jobs as an excuse for them to golf all weekend or be gone hunting, fishing, or indulging in whatever hobby they have, but never allowing their wives to do the same. I know your job can be stressful, but try being a mom. Your wife needs a break, also.

In a Grand and Glorious relationship, both parties need the freedom to pursue their hobbies and spend some time with friends. Equal time and financial resources need to be made available for both of you. Obviously, there are a few ground rules that should be adhered to. We must recognize every human is vulnerable to some degree. No one should put themselves in a compromising situation. Be smart. Don't have any secrets from each other. Honesty and openness are a must.

Don't smother your partner. I have known people in relationships where one party will not let the other out of their sight. This is unhealthy. We all need our space. The only logical reasons for smothering are insecurity or a lack of trust. Either way, counseling is needed to get to the root of the problem.

Freedom to grow and develop your interests and hobbies will be extremely valuable the longer you are in a relationship. As your children grow up and move out, you both need to have friends and hobbies to help fill the void that is left. Working together over the years and encouraging each other to pursue your passions will strengthen your friendship and keep your relationship strong. Where there is love and trust, there is freedom.

The last "F word" is forgiveness. We are all going to need forgiveness from time to time. Often, I am a little too blunt. I say things I shouldn't, in a way I shouldn't. When I do, I need to know I can ask for forgiveness from Linda and get it.

When we forgive, we need to drop it. Do not use the situation as a weapon. It is also essential that when we ask for and receive forgiveness, we are grateful for it and strive to avoid needing forgiveness for the same thing over and over again. If we have a problem in a certain area, we need to work on it.

Forgiveness is like love; it is a choice. Just like I choose to love someone, I have to choose to forgive. On the cross, Jesus asked God to forgive the people who were crucifying Him. The word He used for forgiveness meant to forgive without punishment. Verbalizing forgiveness while wishing or praying the person we are forgiving will be punished is not forgiveness. Forgiveness is setting the other person free. It also sets us free. Harboring unforgiveness will destroy us.

Sadly, not everyone can receive forgiveness, just like not everyone can receive love. We all know someone who has been so hurt that they just can't seem to let themselves be loved or forgiven.

Sometimes, they have something in their past that won't allow them to forgive themselves. If not dealt with, this mindset will cause them to self-destruct. Thankfully, God's mercy endures forever; someday they will be made whole and restored.

Remember, you can't fix anyone but yourself. You can love and forgive, but you cannot change anyone. You may end up in a situation where you need to accept that, forgive yourself, and move on.

Chapter 6

Learn to Say "No"

My word for 2023 was "No!" It was based upon Matthew 5:37 – "Let your word or thought be Yes and mean Yes, or No and let No end the matter. Anything else brings hard labor and pain."

So often in life, we get ourselves into a mess because we say yes to something we don't want to do instead of just saying no. The feelings that follow are similar to buyer's remorse! We regret not saying no.

I have to admit this is an area I struggle with. I hate telling people no. I guess deep down, I'm a people pleaser. I enjoy making others happy. To a point, that's a good thing;

sacrificing some of our time or resources is good, and that's what Jesus did on the cross -- He sacrificed his life to show us God's love for us. It is good for me to give up some of my time to help others and do things with my family or friends that they want to do. On the other hand, sometimes, I commit to things that take time away from those people or things most important to me, my family, my employees, or my business. When I do so, I find myself frustrated over the situation, which is no one's fault but mine.

Learning to say no is hard for some of us, but we have to learn how to say no to be happy. Here are a few insights that are helping me.

First, I ask myself if saying no will damage my relationship with the person asking. If so, am I ok with that? In some cases, that answer might need to be, "Yes, I am ok with damaging the relationship." Some relationships are unhealthy; they occupy our time, energy, and resources but never contribute to our well-being. We probably all have relationships that only take from us. Saying no may be ok in this case. In the long run, it might help that relationship become healthy by making the other party realize they have been using you while never giving anything back to the relationship.

Second, am I saying no because I am selfish or because saying yes will take time away from something more important? Time is valuable; we have plenty of it, but only if we use it wisely. How many times have you gotten on social media or turned on the TV and wasted 30 minutes to an hour of your life? I'm not saying those things are evil, or you should never do them, but when you do, it needs to be because you don't have something more important to do at the time.

Third, can I stick to the decision and be at peace with myself if I say no? Once I say no, I need to give up all rights to criticize, critique, or meddle in the situation.

Finally, if I don't say no but instead say yes, I need to accept that I no longer have the right to complain about saying yes. I need to have a good attitude and give the situation my best. Few things are more annoying than spending time with someone who is whining because they would prefer to be doing something else! If that's the case, they should have said no in the first place! Let's try hard not to be that person.

Chapter 7

Be Kind

Being kind should be one of the easiest traits to exhibit, yet it is one of the areas I struggle with the most.

I am convinced that a deep, meaningful relationship is impossible without kindness. I don't believe there is any other emotion or action that receives a more positive reaction than kindness.

After 45 years together, one of the things that continues to draw me to her is her kindness. She has an amazing way of caring for people, and her kindness towards her family and friends makes me a better person.

I think it is fair to say that most of us struggle with being kind at times, especially when we don't get our way. The key to being kind is to be kind no matter the circumstance. The Bible says God's loving kindness or mercy endures forever. I believe that. I know it's not the popular thing to say, still, I really do believe God's mercy and loving-kindness endure forever, and no matter how screwed up we are or what we do, God is unwilling to give up on us. Because of this, I have decided that I need to be as kind as I can be.

What are some ways we can be kind in our relationship? In marriage, we could (men) wash the dishes, start the washer, load the dryer, and put away the clothes. Guess what, guys? The less time your wife has to spend doing these things, the more time she can spend with you!

My wife and I are pretty good at this. We both work and have very busy schedules, so one of us might load the dishwasher and the other put up the dishes. One might run a load of clothes, and the other might throw those clothes in the dryer and start another load.

Being kind is simply doing something for someone that improves their life; it can be a kind word, a gesture, a note, or a hug. We do it for someone, not because of obligation but because we know it makes their day better, and that, my friends, is a powerful thing. Your small acts of kindness can have a big impact on someone's day, and ultimately, on your relationship. Telling someone how much you love them or care for them is important, but actually doing something for them without being asked means even more.

Let me share with you why I feel kindness is so valuable. As I mentioned, God's loving kindness endures forever. He uses it to show us how much he cares for us. We are told He uses His loving kindness to make us aware of our imperfections and flaws. We are also told His love is a consuming fire. Many people misuse the word "consuming" to say to us He is going to destroy or torment us with fire. Sadly, that is a total lie based upon Pagan teachings introduced into the Bible around 440 B.C. The word translated as "consuming" actually means purifying. Maybe this is where the phrase "kill-um with kindness" comes from, but one thing I know for sure is that God will pursue us with loving kindness until we finally understand He only wants what's best for us. I am convinced that pursuing our partner with loving kindness benefits us both.

Chapter 8

Be Generous

"Give, and it shall be given unto you..."

– Jesus (Luke 6:36)

I believe this to be one of the most profound statements ever uttered. In a world that seems so focused on take, take, take, the real answer in life is give, give, give.

Being generous can take on many forms. We must give our time, energy, emotions, and resources in a relationship. Our relationship will suffer if we are stingy in any of these areas.

Over the years, I have witnessed many marriages lacking generosity from either one or both parties. The result is often a long-term marriage that is more of a business partnership than a marriage. In a marriage, when we are not generous with each other, we will find different ways to satisfy our needs. This could be an outside relationship with another person, but more often, it is with hobbies or other interests. Maybe this works for some, but I can't help but believe it pales in comparison to a kind, generous, truthful relationship with the person you loved enough to marry.

Studies show that the giver in a relationship tends to love more than the receiver. If only one person gives, two things will happen over time: the receiver will become expectant and ungrateful, and the giver will begin to feel unappreciated and resentful.

Teaching our kids early in life to give and to be grateful when they receive will help them be successful in all they do. I would encourage you to make them write thank you cards for birthday and Christmas gifts. This will help them be aware of the time someone took to buy a gift for them, and yes, I said make them! Learning to do things that are inconvenient and require a little effort will benefit them.

When I give, I always feel gratification. I have learned to give without looking for something in return, but I can honestly say that every time I give, I seem to get a blessing in return, normally from a totally unexpected source.

Imagine what the world would be like if we all became better givers. I'm not just talking about money. I'm also talking about love, time, and kindness. Imagine if we, as individuals, began truly putting our families ahead of our jobs, hobbies, and social activities.

I often talk with young people who feel their parents care more about things than them. I know you must work to provide, but it may be as William Paul Young once said, we need to realize that the "opposite of more is enough!" Nurturing, teaching values, and helping our families through life are much more important than things.

Giving ourselves to our families and our neighborhood first will create more value than giving to most charities would. Understand, I am not anti-charities; I give to several. I do, however, try to research their effectiveness before I give. The point I am trying to make is that sometimes we donate to charities because it makes us feel good about our-selves, and giving money is much easier than grinding it out daily in our own backyard.

I am not opposed to these institutions; they can offer ex-cellent services, but the reality is if we, as individuals across the world, focused more on the needs of those we live with or are near, the need for many of the charities that exist would go away.

The government is not good at providing day-to-day services; that's not why it exists. Local governments could provide money for mental health and drug treatment cen-ters; however, it has been my experience that when the gov-ernment gets involved, it typically does more harm than good due to red tape and silly rules.

I have seen many good charities go downhill after agree-ing to accept government funding. As I look around, I see churches spend hundreds of millions of dollars to build gymnasiums, fellowship halls, and bowling alleys while our streets are filled with homeless people and our communi-ties are full of people living in poverty. I know there are ex-ceptions, but I think you will have to agree the average homeless person would not be welcome in the average church. I encourage you to find places to give your time and money where you feel like a real difference is being made in the lives of those in need.

In your marriage, give your partner the things they need from you. In the series New Amsterdam, Max always asked "How can I help?" This has made an impact on how I interact with people. I am learning that when I ask this question sincerely, people respond positively. If you are unsure of what your partner needs, ask them. Encourage them to be truthful with their response. When they are truthful, it may hurt; if so, take a minute and soak it in to see why. Maybe they have a good point, which is why it bothers you! Don't respond in anger. Listen, agree to consider what they have said, then meditate on it to see if there is truth. You will never go wrong by listening. If you own a business, give your customers the best possible service and your employees the best possible working environment. If you are an employee, give your employer the very best job performance you can. Treat customers with dignity and respect. If you're a customer, treat the employees at the business you're dealing with respectfully. We all have bad days. Sometimes, a kind word or a generous tip can totally change someone's day or life.

One thing I am sure of is you will never regret becoming generous. I believe with all my heart that being generous will change your outlook on life; we were created to be givers. Don't miss out on the blessings that are yours.

Chapter 9

Be Truthful

How many times in life have you looked back at a situation and thought how much different it could have been had everyone just been truthful? Truthfulness in this day and age seems to be a lost trait. Politicians lie to us, the media is deceitful, and social platforms manipulate the truth. Sometimes, it's hard to know just who we can trust. This is why it is so crucial that we be honest with those closest to us. We all need someone we can depend on to be truthful with us. Truthfulness is freeing and comforting to us. We can handle almost anything as long as we are confident it is true.

Honesty in a relationship is so vital. Once your partner knows they can trust you to be truthful with them, your relationship will move to a whole new level. I should probably clarify that our truthfulness must be coupled with kindness! The way we say something can sometimes be just as important as what we say. "Honey, that dress distracts from your beauty" is much better than "you look fat in that dress."

Being truthful about your feelings, thoughts, and desires while at the moment may cause a little discomfort, but I promise, in the long run, it will be better. Not being truthful just prolongs or postpones a greater conflict. In business, marriage, or family, the sooner we get to the truth of an issue, the better off everyone is. Most major blowups occur because minor issues weren't dealt with in a timely manner.

So often, I see people supposedly trying to protect their spouse by sheltering them from the truth. It has been my experience that, in reality, they just don't want to be honest about the situation because they are embarrassed or afraid to own up to what they perceive as a weakness. In other words, they are protecting themselves by not facing reality.

My advice is to be open and honest about things. Delaying the truth will not make the situation better, but it may very well make it worse. When we are lied to or deceived, it becomes difficult to trust again. Losing someone's trust is easy, but regaining it is very hard. It is not impossible, but it is hard. Remember that when you are teetering on telling the truth.

Learning to be truthful with kindness will be one of the most freeing, satisfying experiences of your life. When we suppress or hide our true feelings it drags us down and wears us out, making us defensive and unhappy. I want to emphasize again that our truthfulness must be laced with kindness, if it's not, it can be just as cruel as dishonesty. Everything we do must be done with kindness, especially truthfulness.

Sometimes in life, family or friends will try to guilt us into participating in their stupidity. We are not obligated to do so, no matter how much they try to convince us that we are. If someone is totally convinced that they want to live in a certain way, that is their choice. They are free to do so as long as their lifestyle does not infringe upon ours and require us to alter ours. For example, if a relative or friend chooses not to work because they need a break, that's great, unless their way to do that is for them and their cat and dog to live with us in our house. Don't be afraid to say no. Sometimes, the only way we can become aware of our stupidity is to be told no.

We have lots of excuses for not being truthful. In my old age, I am coming to believe that if the truth damages the relationship, the relationship wasn't that great to start with, and it's best to get it out in the open now. By doing so, you might eliminate one of those areas in your life that you find yourself saying yes to when, in fact, you want to say no!

Chapter 10

Fight Fair

Every relationship is going to have disagreements. Anytime two people are involved, there will be differing opinions. Some of them will be minor and not really matter in the grand scope of life. I may prefer apple pie over coconut cream, my steak medium rare versus well done, hot weather to cold. While it may be challenging to plan a vacation with someone whose preferences for these things differ from mine, these obstacles are pretty easy to overcome with very little effort on either person's side. We should be able to have a little fun with these things, but they shouldn't cause any major conflict.

My wife and I have a great relationship. We laugh a lot together, enjoy life, and sometimes argue! After 45 years of marriage, we know each other pretty well. It's rare anymore that we totally disagree on something—rare—but not out of the realm of possibility!

Over 45 years, we have had a few "knockdown, drag-out" arguments. Emotionally, not physically! We are both very confident and vocal about our opinions. That's why I love her so much. I usually know what she is thinking, and I don't have to spend days or hours trying to figure out what is wrong, but still, from time to time a situation will arise that we butt heads on. As I said, these are rare now, but they still happen.

Neither of us is good at dropping issues and punting them down the road. We both prefer a conclusion to a problem. We do, though, go about it differently. She is a head-on, "let's fix this right now!" personality, I am a head-on, "let's fix this after I replay it through my mind and calm down" personality. She doesn't get angry very often, but if I'm not careful, I can let it fly! This is why she can normally deal with an issue here and now, and I may need a few hours or days to gather my thoughts before confronting it. Neither approach is wrong; it's just how we are wired.

Early in marriage, this could cause an issue. My wife wanted to deal with the situation right now so she could sleep, and I needed to sleep on it so I could deal with it properly. Over time, thankfully, we learned to understand each other, and we have been able to compromise. I can let her express her issue and listen to her. She can let me digest the situation before I respond, because she knows I will deal with it once I have some time to think about it.

The key is that in every healthy relationship, there will be times when we disagree. That is okay. We are human, we are emotional, and we have opinions. A good argument now and then is okay. It's how we handle it that matters.

I remember hearing about a young woman, in tears, calling her mother-in-law to let her know that she and her new husband were getting a divorce. Shocked, her mother-in-law asked why. The woman responded, "Well, we had a fight this morning before he left for work, so I guess we will be getting a divorce." Apparently, her parents had never argued in front of her, so she assumed an argument meant a divorce.

I share this to let you know that arguing in front of your kids is okay. In fact, I believe it's beneficial for them, provided you fight fairly; let them see you make peace and explain that disagreements are a part of life. Use those situations to teach them how to resolve conflict. Obviously, some conflicts should not be dealt with in front of your children, especially if it is about them personally. It is important to use constraint and good judgment.

Here are a few rules for fighting fair:

1. Stay as calm as possible.
2. If the neighbors can hear you, you are forgetting Rule #1.
3. Words matter. You can't take them back. Guard them closely.
4. Don't compare. "You're just like your mom" (or brother or dad) are trigger words that will cause your partner to react instead of listen.
5. Don't bring up their past by saying things like "You always," or "Remember last time…"
6. Work for a resolution.
7. Kiss and make up. Hold each other. Let your kids see you. If you can't do this, you haven't resolved the issue.

Chapter 11

Learn to Laugh

"A lot of times, men say, 'I wish women would come with instructions,' but do you know any men who *ever* read instructions?" – Yakov Smirnoff

Laughing is a great healer. We have to be able to laugh at ourselves and each other. Folks, we are funny creatures; we do some really dumb stuff. Unless we can laugh about it, we will always be wounded.

Laughter relieves tension by helping us relax. The benefits from this are staggering. Here are a few I found from different studies.

1. Laughter is a natural painkiller. It releases endorphins, which soothe stress and reduce anxiety.
2. Laughter strengthens your heart by accelerating your heartbeat.
3. Laughter wards off disease by boosting the immune system.
4. Laughter tones your abs. Laughing 10-15 minutes a day can cause you to burn 40 calories per day.
5. Laughter lightens anger's load.
6. Laughter decreases blood pressure.
7. Laughter helps you live longer. A Norwegian study found that people with a sense of humor lived longer. This was particularly notable in those battling cancer.
8. Laughter helps with depression by lightening your mood.

I think most of us have experienced times when laughter eased our pain or stress in the middle of a really hard moment. I read somewhere that watching a few minutes of comedy each day does wonders for our health and mental outlook. I miss The Three Stooges, Burns & Allen, and Red

Skelton. They had the ability to make us laugh and, for a few minutes, forget our problems. They weren't political, they weren't nasty, they were just funny.

In a relationship, there must be laughter. Show me a relationship without it, and I will show you a relationship that is in big trouble.

I mentioned the comedian Dr. Yakov Smirnoff in an earlier chapter. After going through a divorce, he went back to school and got his master's and PhD in Psychology. His focus was on relationships. He shares that he knew his marriage was over when his wife no longer laughed at his jokes. In his studies, he discovered that men and women are different. Men want physical intimacy, to be admired for things they do, and a recreational companion. Women want affection, conversation, and family commitment. In his song, "Far from Me," John Prine shares these lyrics, "Why we used to laugh together, and we'd dance to any old song, well, ya know, she still laughs with me, but she waits just a second too long."

If your relationship has lost its laughter, you need to do your best to regain it. Seek counseling. Think back to things that made you laugh, the activities that brought enjoyment, the places that allowed you to relax and have fun. Don't wait until it's too late. Do whatever it takes to rebuild your friendship. Don't allow yourself or your partner to become comfortable in your complacency!

To keep laughter in your relationship, you have to be able to laugh at yourself. As I pointed out earlier, we all say and do some pretty stupid stuff. Being able to acknowledge it and laugh about it is of the utmost importance. Always laughing at the other person and never at yourself will create conflict over time. Laughter has to be a two-way street. Trust is hard to come by in a relationship where we can't laugh at ourselves, admit our mistakes, and move on.

Chapter 12

Keep It Fresh

In 1980, I attended a conference featuring Ernie "Tex" Prichard. That experience helped shape how I have lived my family life more than any other event. I was 22 then, newly married, trying to figure out life.

Tex shared about the importance of vacationing. He told us that he and his wife always took vacations each year with their kids. He told some of the stories from their trips. They weren't quite as bad as Chevy Chase's Vacation, but there were several mishaps! It was hard work for him and his wife to plan and carry out the trips. At times, they seemed like a disaster, but there were always lots of great memories when they were done. At the time of this conference, his kids were grown, and he pointed out that each of them still talked about those vacations and the fun they had. They had forgotten the mishaps, but they remembered the great experiences, much like the scene in *National Lampoon's Christmas Vacation* when Clark asked his dad how he always seemed to make the holidays go so smoothly without a glitch. His dad explained how they really weren't that smooth; besides he said, "I always had a little help from Jack Daniel's." There were plenty of mishaps, but again, the point is that we tend to remember the good and forget the bad.

In addition to taking family vacations, Tex stressed the importance of taking vacations without the kids. All couples need time together to relax, refresh, and renew. These trips don't have to be grandiose, but they do need to happen. My wife and I were blessed to have good mothers. Although they lived 200 miles away, they were willing to help us out and watch the kids while we vacationed. Our first vacation without our oldest son was when he was nine months old. Parents, the kids will survive a few days without you. In fact, they will probably do better because you will be in a better mood!

Remember, vacations don't have to be 10-day cruises. Some of our kids' fondest memories were from our simplest trips. Sometimes, we never even left town. We would check in to a local hotel with a nice indoor pool. During the day, we would go to the zoo, watch a movie, go to the mall, or go to an amusement park. The point is that we were disconnected from the day-to-day and connected to each other.

Another way to keep it fresh is to avoid routines as much as possible. While structure is good, it can also be monotonous—and cause boredom and complacency. It's definitely not what we want when we are trying to keep our relationship fresh and playful. Remember, relationships take work. Men, I am especially speaking to you right now. So many times, I see men fail to step it up and help out with their kids, and they can't figure out why their wives are too tired for them. Men, wake up! If you want more "alone time" with your wife, to quote Cousin Eddy, turn off the TV, get out of your chair, and help out around the house.

During my years as a leader of Divorce Caree groups, I learned several things. One of the most enlightening was the fact that the top three most significant years for divorce are year 1, year 6, and year 25 of marriage. Year 1 being on the list made sense to me because I realized sometimes people just get into a marriage and aren't ready for it. Year 6's appearance didn't surprise me that much either due to the probability of learning how to adjust to having young children running around the house. The 25th year being on that list, though, was a shocker. You would think that by then, couples would have it figured out. Here's what I hadn't initially thought about, possibly because neither I nor my peers had reached this stage yet: around the 25th year of marriage, kids are moving out, going to college, getting married, or going to work, and all of a sudden, we are alone with a stranger because we have not kept our relationship fresh. Our focus has been on our careers and kids; we have not grown together but separately. We no longer know how to relate to each other one-on-one. Folks, let me make this clear: unless your kids have a physical or an emotional restraint, they are not going to live with you forever, so you need to accept that now and make sure your partner is your first priority. You cannot have a healthy relationship and healthy kids if you put your kids first. I know that's not popular, but it is true. The stronger your relationship, the more likely you will have strong, resourceful kids.

My wife and I love to take trips together. It doesn't really matter where we go; we just like to get away by ourselves. Don't get me wrong, we love to travel with our family and friends, but we enjoy our trips with just the two of us. We have taken many cruises from 7-21 days. Each time, we would have gotten right back on the boat and gone again. We have friends who think we're nuts. They can't imagine being together for that long in confined quarters. We can't imagine anything better. The important thing is to do fun stuff together. Whatever it is that you enjoy doing together, make time for it. I'm convinced we have plenty of time to do what we want if we are willing to say no to things that aren't important and don't strengthen our relationship or add value to our lives.

This past spring, we were in Flagstaff, Arizona, celebrating my birthday. It was late March, so we knew it was a crapshoot on whether or not I would get any golf in. We also knew an hour's drive would put us in sunny, warm weather. When we arrived, most of the snow on the course where we were staying had melted, and it looked like it would open up while we were there. The first couple of days were very nice. We went to the Grand Canyon, which was absolutely beautiful. We had seen it from the Vegas side and had done a helicopter tour, but the views from this side were gorgeous. We hiked, shopped, and had a great time. On the way back to Flagstaff, it began to snow. We woke up the next morning to 6" of snow. Although it was beautiful, we decided it would hamper our plans. We looked at the map and weather for different areas, and 2 hours later, we were in the car and on our way to Vegas. Linda called and got us a room, and I made a couple of tee times. A few hours later, I was on the links! We hung out for a couple of days. I golfed, we shopped, invested a few dollars in the local economy, and then headed back to Flagstaff to rest up before flying home.

Being flexible makes life so much more enjoyable. Learn to relax, have fun and be in the moment. It's good to plan ahead, but don't let a glitch in your plans stop you from making the most of each day!

Chapter 13

Take care of yourself!

One of my dearest friends was a cowboy preacher, Boyce Evans. Boyce had the ability to tell it straight and not make you mad. When it came to relationships, he had an old saying, "Wives, don't let your husband come home to a pigpen with a pig in it." Ladies, before you get too offended, I assure you he was just as tough on the men. He has been dead for several years but, 20 years ago he believed that one reason for the rise in singleness and the increasing divorce rate was because men aren't men anymore. Many are content to let their wives be the breadwinner, raise the kids, and do the housework while they sit on the couch and watch TV or hang with their buddies. This chapter will be hard to digest, but I think it needs to be said.

If you enter into a new relationship, I encourage you to predetermine that you will do your best to stay in as good physical shape as possible. I realize health issues can change things, but I also realize that many of our health issues are directly related to our physical condition. When my wife and I got married, I weighed about 145 lbs. I was 21, active in sports, and had great metabolism. As the years passed, I became less active; my metabolism changed, life became stressful with kids and work, and I weighed 185 lbs before long. Although I carried that weight pretty well, I could tell I needed to cut back. I began having back issues. Tying my shoes was a chore. My energy level was low. I knew it was time to do something.

I tried several different diets and exercise over the next few years. Each worked fine for a while until I got bored. Soon, I would put all the weight back on. I finally realized that fad diets and short-term periods of excessive workouts really only made it worse. Eventually, I tried the keto diet. As a whole, it was pretty easy to stick to. What's not to like about lots of meat? For a little over a year, I followed it very closely. It worked. I got down to 160. My wife asked me not to lose any more weight and a Catholic priest friend of mine pulled me aside to see if I was ok. So slowly, I started adding a few things back into my diet. My ideal weight seems to be 168-170. I can tell when I break that number.

For me, cutting back on or eliminating bread, ice cream, and potatoes does the trick. We are all different. We each need to figure it out for ourselves, but we need to figure it out. Shedding a few pounds saves our knees, our heart, and reduces the chance of diabetes. Just a little discipline can make a huge difference.

In addition to diet, we need to exercise. I'm not talking about hours in the gym or miles on your bike; those are fine if that's what floats your boat, but I realize that for most people those things are neither practical or desirable. We are just too busy. On the other hand we all can make time for some type of exercise. It's been my experience that any kind of consistent movement will help.

This is what I have found to help me the most. When I wake up in the mornings, I try to lay still for a few minutes and just be grateful for life. Once up, I drink a glass of water, grab a cup of coffee, and head to my back porch if it's nice out or to my recliner if it's cold. I try to spend about an hour reading, praying, reflecting, and preparing for the day. After that, I spend a few minutes stretching and doing a few exercises. I have found some low-impact exercises that don't hurt my back. Stretching helps my back and balance, and exercising boosts my metabolism. After that I eat breakfast and get ready for work. Again, this is my routine. Yours will be different. A couple of things that I would encourage you to be adamant about are don't jump out of bed, be sure to drink water soon after you get up (this helps activate internal organs), reflect on the things you should be grateful for, and allow yourself plenty of time to get around. I read once that 9 AM is the most likely time to have a heart attack. The article said it was due to getting up too quickly after lying flat all night, a lack of hydration, and rushing around because we are late. Seems plausible to me. Besides, you will be much happier when you don't start the day off rushed.

Take the stairs. Walk as far out of the way as possible. Move. Do something. Sitting around is the absolute worst thing you can do. Don't make excuses. There are diets and exercises for almost all of us. There are actually some designed to do while sitting. Brian Swift, a great author and motivational speaker, works out in his wheelchair. Search until you find a program that works for you. Make a commitment. Stick to it. Watch your diet. Little changes can make a big difference. See yourself the way you want to look and feel. Every morning, take a few minutes and visualize yourself healthy, strong, and happy, then do what it takes to help you achieve your vision.

My desire is to keep myself in the best condition I can and give my wife the closest person to who she married for as long as I possibly can. Staying in shape gives me the best chance of doing that. A few simple disciplines can make a world of difference. Don't wait like I did; start now. Create habits that keep you strong and healthy. As Willie and Merle sang, "We'd of taken much better care of ourselves if we'd known we was gonna live this long." At 90, Willie still bikes, swims, and does taekwondo. Keep a positive attitude, and find a way to exercise, read, and meditate. These habits will be the best medicine you will ever take. Hopefully, we'll all get old. It will be much more fun doing so if we're in decent shape!

Staying fit physically, mentally, emotionally, and spiritually is the best gift I can give my partner, my children, and myself!

Conclusion

I hope that after reading this book, you will truly decide to focus on being kind, generous, and truthful! No matter where you are in life, these three traits will help you have a more enjoyable life. They are not traits that can be mastered, as in reaching a pinnacle in one of them, but rather traits that can become a part of our true being, constantly growing in each of them. They are traits we can pass on to our children, grandchildren, and friends.

Every day, I witness at least one of the areas discussed in this book in real life, sometimes in my own, and other times in the lives of those around me. I am amazed at how often I break my own rules in my relationships. Just this weekend, I was a complete ass to my wife when I should have been understanding. The reality was that I was irritated at some of my employees for doing a poor job. Instead of calling them on a weekend and letting them worry, I fretted about it and allowed myself to be in a bad mood. It reminded me of another Tex Prichard story. He once had a salesman who couldn't sell anything. He had five kids and Tex knew the man wasn't going to be able to provide for them in this profession. Tex would lay awake at night worrying about how to make the guy successful. He finally realized it wasn't his responsibility to provide for the guy's family. He had done all he could to train the guy, but the guy just wasn't cut out to be a car salesman. At 2 a.m. one morning, as he lay awake worrying about it, he phoned the guy and told him, "It's not my responsibility to lay awake at night and worry about how you are going to feed your family, it's yours." I know for some of you, that seems harsh, but life is tough. The realization of being out of work motivated the man to go to work. A few years later, he was the president of a little company known as Dairy Queen! All he needed was someone to push him out of the nest and force him to fly.

I hope you will accept this book as a push out of your comfort zone (nest), take responsibility for your attitude, actions, and accountability and really work on the things outlined in this book; they will make a difference. I am totally confident about that. I have seen them work in my life and the relationships of many others. The worst thing we can do is let our relationships grow stagnant and mundane. Work to keep them fresh, interesting, and relevant. Over the years, I have known many people in failed relationships, and none of them set out with a predetermined plan for their relationship to die; it died because it wasn't tended to by both parties.

I know there will be some of you who will say, you know, I gave it my best shot and it still didn't work. I realize that might be true. Sometimes, we work really hard at something and it still fails. That is part of life. The key is though, we can walk away knowing we did our best and that, in and of itself, should give us the peace we need to go on to the next stage in life. It's when we didn't give it our best that we have regrets. If you have been in a failed relationship, all I can tell you is, that's in the past, you may not be able to fix it. You can, however, make sure you don't repeat the past and work to ensure yourself a bright future. I'm convinced we're never too old to learn, and it's never too late to improve ourselves! Growing in any area of our lives is quite rewarding! It is not our responsibility to change anyone else. Our responsibility is to change ourselves. Many times, as we grow, the people close to us grow also because they like what they see in us. Like most things in life, when we do something good or positive, there are beneficial side effects. Considerate, self-motivated, unselfish, and caring people tend to attract more of the same. I know you will never be disappointed by striving to become a better human being!

Together, let's change our families, businesses, and communities. Being kind, generous, and truthful is contagious.

Have a Grand and Glorious Relationship!

About the Author

Brett and his wife Linda have lived in Oklahoma for 43 years. They are blessed with two great sons, a wonderful daughter-in-law, five grandchildren (4 in Oklahoma and 1 waiting for them in heaven), and are looking forward  to adding an additional daughter-in-law next year!

Together, they have had the great fortune to pour love and encouragement into the lives of many people.

While they both love people of all ages, Linda is especially blessed with the ability to care for and help the aged, while Brett's heart is with young adults. They both love children and babies!

Brett's passion is helping people learn to live in harmony with each other and God, helping them to know God's goodness as Jesus taught us, and teaching people the value of being kind, generous, and truthful.

He believes focusing on these three traits can truly lead you to Grand and Glorious Relationships.

Brett can be contacted for media appearances and bulk orders at Brett@sparksbixby.com, and he can also be found sharing messages of hope on Facebook and across social media at Brett Neil.